QUIET!
MOMMY'S ASLEEP!

by
Bil Keane

FAWCETT GOLD MEDAL • NEW YORK

QUIET! MOMMY'S ASLEEP!

A Fawcett Gold Medal Book published by arrangement
with The Register & Tribune Syndicate, Inc.

ISBN 0-449-13930-1

Printed in the United States of America

10 9 8 7 6 5

"I'm one grade older now!"

"I'm lonely!"

"It doesn't sound like the ocean to me—it sounds like a lawn mower."

"Every time I run around on a hot day my face leaks."

"Mommy can teach you to tie 'em, Daddy—she knows how."

"Mommy! Kittycat caught a bird and brought it home to show us! Is she good or bad?"

"What do you want for lunch?"

"Mommy, God's here!"

"Which Grandma is it? The one that wears lipstick or
the other one?"

"I'll bet you'd scold me if I put my thumb in a pie."

"Mommy! The pool's gettin' wet!"

"I think I'm getting seesaw-sick."

"Don't worry, Daddy — the next picture is for you!"

"Anyway, I'm more a member of this family than you
are — I was BORNED into it, but you only
married into it."

"I could stay as clean as you do if I wasn't down here so close to the ground."

"Mr. Strack, you have a hole in your hair."

"Mommy, tell Billy to stop imitating a frog 'cause I'm tired of it!"

"A super-burger, three french fries, one large coke, a
small root beer . . . No, that's TWO french fries,
TWO large cokes . . . make it THREE . . ."

"MOMMY! It's the ninth point of the tie-breaker and Daddy's serving! WANNA WATCH?"

"If Mommy was here I'd really cry up a storm."

"The snake ate all the
peanuts!"

"Look, Mommy! We can make it snow in the sum-
mertime."

"I'd love to be a princess, Daddy. Do you think you could get a job as king of someplace?"

"Mommy, I'm happy at you!"

"Here's one that hasn't hatched yet."

"I just washed my hands yesterday and they're dirty again already."

"Grandma, how come I never win when I play with Billy, but when I play with you I ALWAYS win?"

"I wish we had named Sam a GIRL'S name so we could have some puppies."

"Now don't break.it!"

"MARCO ... POLO! MARCO ... POLO! MARCO
... POLO! MARCO ... POLO!"

"Will you take my turns for me, Mommy? I want to
play outside for a while."

"I SEE A FISH, DADDY! I SEE A FISH!"

"How do you know MY friends did the tee-peeing?"

"We're collectin' bugs and PJ is the bait."

"I can't take a nap today — Kittycat's usin' my bed."

"I want the hamburger and french fries, but do I
have to ask for the 'Little Miss Muffet'?"

"Daddy, how long does it take for a muscle to grow?"

"The only thing I don't know about playin' tennis is
how to hold the bat."

"We're watching '20,000 Legs Under the Sea.'"

"PJ learned a new word . . . from the plumber."

"I don't want to read that book-- I'll wait for the movie."

"I took the bang-aid off myself, Mommy! I think I'm
going to be a doctor!"

"And if you so much as set foot in the street, you'll march right up to your room!"

"I'm gonna give this one to Grandma and she won't even have to PAY me for it."

"That's a LADY BUG."
"How can you tell?"

"Mommy was in my dream last night, weren't you, Mommy?"

"Why did Mr. Allen say the scenery's nice? I don't see any scenery."

"It isn't like a lollipop. You can't take your time."

"When I get bigger and live in my own house, will a mother move in with me?"

"You can see what's inside through the teeth holes."

"Mommy, will BLUE socks go with this outfit okay?"

"She called us a party of six! Does that mean we're
going to have a party?"

"Daddy's wipin' the car with my good ol' shirt!"

"Mommy, will you tuck in my ham?"

"Poor Daddy — you won't have anybody to help
you unpack when you get to New York."

"If you get lost, Daddy, you know your name, address and phone number, don't you?"

"Daddy only gave us a LITTLE kiss, but look at the long huggin' and kissin' he's giving Mommy."

"He thought you were leavin' with Daddy."

"I get to sleep in Daddy's place with Mommy!"

"How's everything in New York, Daddy? . . . I'm fine
. . . Yes, I'm helpin' her . . . Did you see me
waving when your plane was taking off?
. . . How's the weather there? . . ."

"Daddy said I'm the man of the house and I'm s'posed to be in charge while he's away!"

"Don't be a dummy, Dolly. You can't see New York
City from that window. It's the other way."

"Sure seems quiet around here without Daddy, doesn't it, Mommy?"

"We sure have soup and sandwich for dinner a lot
when Daddy's away on a trip."

"Mommy! This is comin' from New York City! Maybe
we'll see Daddy!"

"Four of those, please!"

"Wave, Mommy! Wave! That might be Daddy's plane!"

"Daddy! Daddy! My mouth is full of kisses for you!"

"Jeffy slept in your place most of the time while you were away, but don't worry — we changed the sheets."

"One of my toes likes roast beef, but the rest of me doesn't."

"Why don't you ask Grandma to kiss it?"

"Mommy, is this my same head?"

"See, you just hit the notes with these wooden lolli-
pops."

"Why do you wear these glasses, Daddy? Everything
looks funny through 'em."

"I'm right here, Mommy, in case you want me for
something!"

"My hand didn't get shooked."

"I feel like a crowd."

"I'm the best one in the class in buttoning."

"Write 'I must sit still'
fifty times."

"Do you want periods?"

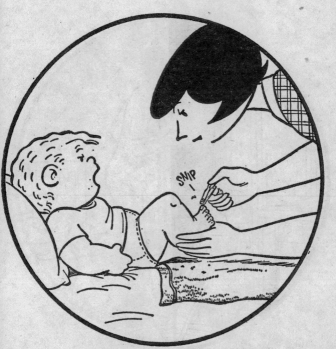

"Did you get us new socks?"

"I'm testin' to see if my new raincoat works."

"I think the cake wants me to eat some of it."

"Daddy, I like it when Mommy's playin' tennis and
you cook the dinner."

"You're lucky PJ — you don't have to be a good example to ANYBODY!"

"I used up all my sleep."

"You need a good
spanking."

"You need a good
kiss."

"It's okay to eat 'em, Jeffy — they're not REAL
ladies' fingers!"

"Mommy, Daddy stepped over me. Does that mean
bad luck?"

"I'd be in trouble if you didn't bring at least one
piece of junk mail each day."

"I'll get something
to write with."

"Mommy, why is this pen
chained to the wall?"

"Would you undo this orange, Mommy?"

"You can't wear it on that finger — that's your
wedding ring finger."

"This is a baby 'm' and this one's a grown-up."

"Why do we have to push our chairs in before·we go
home? We only have to pull them out again
tomorrow."

"Why aren't you dressed as anything, Mommy?"

"All our summer shade is falling down."

"I'm forgettin' my hat, Mommy, so you won't have to shampoo my hair tonight."

"I told Miss Johnson you were mad 'cause she made me stay in at recess. She wants to talk to you."

"Look! That stroller has a baby and a co-baby!"

"No, Barfy! That might be a prince!"

"Must be half time."

"You don't have to wash my arms — I'm gonna
wear a long sleeve shirt."

"I'm starting this letter to Grandma with 'Dear Grandma.' How do you make a 'D,' Mommy?"

"It's easy, PJ! Just let go
and I'll catch you!"

"Mommy, you say 'Umm' and I'll say 'Ahh,' then I'LL
say 'Umm' and YOU say 'Ahh'."

"Why don't you sew a name tag in Daddy's coat like
you do in ours?"

"He hit me, then I hit him, and I hit HIM again and
he hit ME . . . then that's when the fight started."

"Hi, Daddy! I'll carry your grief case!"

"Santa brings us toys and the Easter Bunny brings us candy. What does the Thanksgiving Turkey bring us?"

"Know what I wished? I wished I'd get the BIG piece
of the bone — and it worked!"

"I was quiet in school today. Both the kids that sit
next to me were absent."

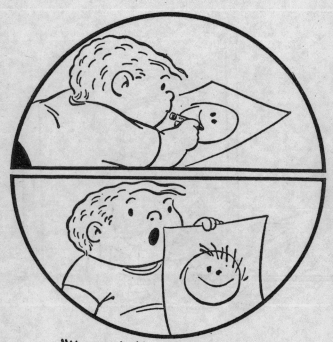

"Mommy, is this anybody we know?"

"That's a five and that's a three and . . ."

"When your Mommy and Daddy made you they
should have made a dog, too."

"Mommy, someday can I wear bracelets on my
teeth?"

"I didn't know horses had their own referees."

"Can you help me find my friend's phone number?
His name is Tommy."

"Let me know when they're ready to be turned on,
Daddy, and I'll flip the switch!"

" ... and may the Christmas spirit which imbues the
hearts of all mankind this joyous season remain
with you and yours throughout
the coming year."
J and B Plumbing, Inc."

"Should I lie Mary down in the straw? She's 'specting a baby y'know."

"Which kind of milk should we put out for Santa —
regular or low fat?"

"I'm gonna open my fire engine first."

"There'll .be nothing else bought around here until Easter!"

HAVE FUN WITH THE FAMILY CIRCUS

I'M TAKING A NAP   14144 · $1.25
LOOK WHO'S HERE!   14207 $1.25
PEACE, MOMMY, PEACE   14145 · $1.25
PEEKABOO! I LOVE YOU!   14174 $1.25
WANNA BE SMILED AT?   14118 $1.25
WHEN'S LATER, DADDY?   14124 $1.25
MINE   14056· $1.25
SMILE!   14172 $1.25
JEFFY'S LOOKIN' AT ME!   14096 $1.25
CAN I HAVE A COOKIE?   14155 $1.25
THE FAMILY CIRCUS   14068 $1.25
HELLO, GRANDMA?   14169 $1.25
I NEED A HUG   14147 $1.25
QUIET! MOMMY'S ASLEEP!   13930 · $1.25

This offer expires 3/13/81   8006-3